THE TEACHING OF
SECRET RAPTURE
IS A
HOAX

METUSELA ALBERT

To order additional copies of this book, contact:
Xlibris
844-714-8691
www.Xlibris.com
Orders@Xlibris.com

Scripture quotations marked KJV are from the Holy Bible, King
James Version (Authorized Version). First published in 1611.
Quoted from the KJV Classic Reference Bible, Copyright © 1983
by The Zondervan Corporation.

ISBN: Softcover   978-1-6698-0457-4
             EBook   978-1-6698-0458-1

Print information available on the last page

Rev. date: 12/15/2021

CONTENT

INTRODUCTION

I often tell others, "When you know the truth, you will easily know the error(s). But if you don't know the truth, you will <u>not</u> know the error(s)."

Just because millions of people believed a certain doctrine to be true, that does <u>not</u> make it true, <u>unless God said it</u> in the Bible.

The Truth is not based on the majority of people who believed a certain teaching from Scripture. Truth will always be the truth because "<u>God said it</u>." Beware of the misinterpretation of Scripture by others.

TEST THE INTERPRETATION BY OTHERS

When you read the Bible, the text must be interpreted correctly in "<u>the context</u>" and "<u>the chronological order</u>." This is an important principle in interpreting Scripture.

For example. When God told Noah to build the Ark because he is going to destroy the world with a flood, the vast majority of the people did <u>not</u> believe that there is going to be a flood since it had never rained before – (Genesis 6:1-10). When the flood happened after 120 years from the time Noah warned them, only eight (8) people believed and entered the Ark *before* rain started to fall. The eight people believed what <u>God told Noah</u>.

Despite the fact that they had not seen rain, the eight people entered the Ark <u>by faith and obedience</u> to what God said. Noah and his wife, and their three sons and their three wives <u>believed</u> what God said, and by <u>FAITH, obeyed</u> God – (Hebrews 11:6-8). They worked together in the building of the Ark and entered the Ark when the time came. Not one of those eight people died during the flood.

God (Yahweh) who created heaven and earth became their protector in the Ark during the time of torrential rain and flood which covered the mountains and the earth. Try and imagine the swift current and the flood waters that swept and destroyed all animals and living things outside the Ark. Unfortunately, millions of people were destroyed by the flood due to misinformation (conspiracy theories), lack of faith and disobedience to God.

From the time of creation to the time of the flood, it was only 1,656 years – (Genesis 5).

THE FINAL SIGN BEFORE THE FLOOD.

Before the flood, God in his mercy gave the people another chance to arouse the minds of the people to think again, that Noah may be correct. What was the final sign?

THE ANIMALS WALKING INTO THE ARK.

Did not this miracle arouse the people's mind to think deeper? . . . There's a super natural power leading the animals into the Ark. The *unclean* animals came from everywhere in one pair, male and female, but the *clean animals* in seven pairs. Who cannot see the miracle? . . .

It is important that we understand what genuine faith is all about. Faith without works (obedience) is death. Obedience is the evidence of faith. Noah's faith was seen by his obedience to God, and he became the heir of righteousness by faith – (Hebrews 11:7). If faith failed to produce obedience, then faith is fake. Remember, faith and works go hand in hand – (James 2:17-25).

Sadly, the millions of people outside the Ark during the flood were lost because they REJECTED the truth. When they rejected the truth, they rejected God who spoke through Noah to build the Ark and warn the people about the coming flood – (Genesis 6:1-10).

WHAT ABOUT OUR TIME?

At the end time *after* the seven last plagues in Revelation 16 when Jesus returns to take his people to heaven, many will be lost because they loved __not__ the truth. And because they loved __not__ the truth, they rejected God; therefore, God will give them a delusion to believe a lie. (2 Thessalonians 2:9-11).

Truth is the truth in the Bible when it is interpreted in the context and in a chronological order of events. Truth is not based on your emotions (your feelings) or by man's interpretation out of context. Please read Isaiah 8:20.

NOTE: This book will present the truth about the second coming of Jesus, and will also expose the lie about the Secret Rapture teaching. When you fully have a good understanding of the return of Jesus, you then will not be fooled again by such twisted teaching called – "The Secret Rapture." Another false expression is – "Left Behind."

Stay tuned to learn something that perhaps you have not understood yet because you have been deceived by others for so long, thus, you are not able to know the truth from the error in regard to this subject. A good detox is necessary to get rid of the toxic among so many Evangelic Christians.

If you have been believing in the teaching of Secret Rapture before the great Tribulation period, I can assure you that you will not believe again in that false doctrine, after reading this book with an open mind. And you must give God the glory for leading you to find this book.

Please share the information and the Book with your friends, etc. They can get this book online www.xlibris.com. Search for the Title and the Author.

May God bless your ministry and family abundantly in good health, spiritually and physically, and in wealth too.

Wish you all a blessed year, 2022.

. . . .

> - # The Secret Rapture Teaching is a COUNTERFEIT of the Return of JESUS.
>
> - # Try and read 1 Thessalonians 4:16-17 and 1 Corinthians 15:52-55.

IF the saints were already taken to heaven by a secret rapture event, then the second coming of JESUS to take the saints <u>does not</u> make sense. Think folks.

CHAPTER 1

WHAT IS THE TEACHING OF SECRET RAPTURE?

The Chart (Diagram) below shows the teaching of the Secret Rapture theory. It says, when the Secret Rapture takes place, it will take <u>seven years</u> for JESUS to return and take the righteous to heaven.

NOTE: Secret Rapture is the belief that the believers in JESUS as the Messiah will be secretly taken to heaven from wherever they are, <u>seven years before the return of JESUS</u>.

It also teaches that three and a half years before the second coming of JESUS, the Anti-Christ in Revelation 13 will appear in Jerusalem.

The Secret Rapture believers advocated that <u>the Great Tribulation</u> will take place three and a half years *after* the Secret Rapture; and three and a half years *before* the return of JESUS.

. . . .

SECRET RAPTURE TAKES PLACE

ANTI-CHRIST APPEARS IN JERUSALEM

RETURN OF JESUS

THREE AND A HALF YEARS

YOU cannot buy OR sell unless you have one of these three things: (1) the name of the Beast, (2) the number of the Beast, or (3) the Mark of the Beast. (Rev. 13:1618).

THREE AND A HALF YEARS

SEVEN YEARS

According to the Secret Rapture teaching, one would know the day and year of the return of JESUS.

How?

Because when the Secret Rapture takes place, it would take another 7 years for the return of JESUS. . . . This doctrine contradicts the Bible.

. . . .

The Evangelical Christians who teach the Secret Rapture doctrine have been fooled for so long. They are the same people who believed that JESUS died at Calvary and changed the Ten Commandments. Though they preached JESUS CHRIST as the Messiah, nevertheless, they have a lot of contradicting messages that support Satan's attack upon JESUS and his law. They mixed truth and error. They failed to realize their many contradictions.

THEIR SECRET RAPTURE DOCTRINE IS A COUNTERFEIT TO DISTORT THE SECOND COMING OF JESUS.

. . . .

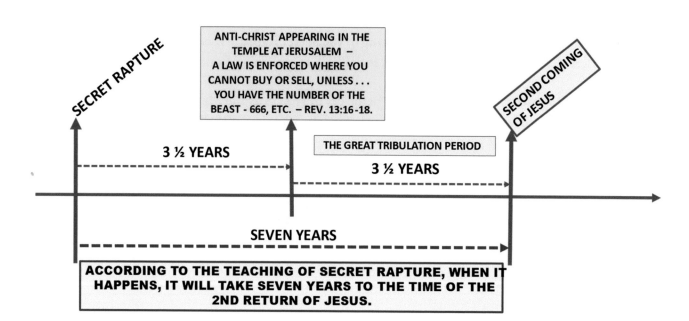

CHAPTER 2

THE <u>FOUR</u> FINAL EVENTS LEADING TO THE SECOND COMING OF JESUS.

Please read and study the chart below of <u>the four final events</u> leading to the Second Coming of JESUS in <u># 5.</u>

. . . .

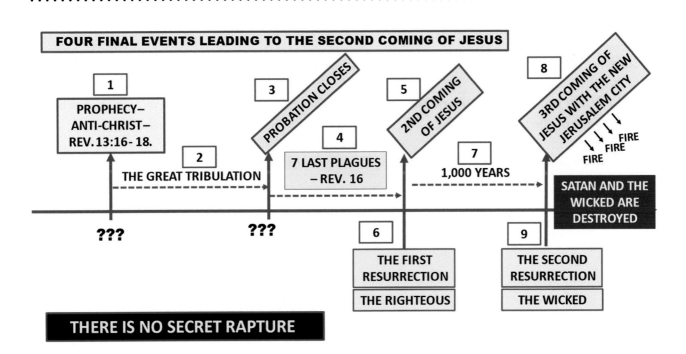

PLEASE take note of events # 6, # 7, # 8, and # 9 in the chart above because that is the context and chronological order of the PLAN OF SALVATION given to us by God (YAHWEH / JEHOVAH) who created us and humbly became incarnated through Mary at Bethlehem (04 B.C.) to pay the penalty of sin at Calvary (31 A.D.).

He who was <u>an everlasting God</u> became human flesh like us to save us. He who was <u>the everlasting Father</u> became the Son of God by incarnation to redeem us from sin and eternal death.

. . . .

THE <u>FOUR EVENTS</u> THAT WILL TAKE PLACE <u>BEFORE</u> THE SECOND COMING OF JESUS.

(See the Chart above).

At the time of writing this book, these events are yet to fulfill in the near future. In fact, the current pandemic (Covid-19) that affected the world is a reminder of the nearness of those events to happen.

Event # 1 – The prophecy given in Revelation 13:16-18 where you cannot buy or sell, etc.

Event # 2 – The Great Tribulation time.

Event # 3 – The Close of Probation.

Event # 4 – The Seven Last Plagues in Revelation 16. (This pandemic will affect the world).

Event # 5 – The Second Coming of Jesus.

NOTE: When you fully understand the sequence of these <u>five events</u> listed above, you then will <u>not</u> believe again in the teaching called – SECRET RAPTURE before the Great Tribulation.

Remember, when you know the truth, you will easily know the error(s).

. . . .

EVENT # 1 – The prophecy in Revelation 13:16-18.

This prophecy is when the nation called America, the lamb like Beast, will speak like a dragon (Revelation 13:1-5), by <u>enforcing</u> a law in the future <u>in support of the BEAST</u>, where you cannot buy or sell <u>unless you have three things</u>:

1. The <u>Name</u> of the Beast.

2. The <u>Number</u> of the Beast's NAME which adds up to 666.

3. The <u>Image</u> and <u>Mark</u> of the Beast.

Remember, the BEAST is <u>a religious organization</u> that Satan gives power to deceive the world. So, have an open mind to guess which church is that? . . . Don't forget, at the time of JESUS on earth, it was <u>the Jewish Church</u> that orchestrated his crucifixion by <u>the Roman government at Calvary.</u>

First, we must find out who the BEAST is, in order to know his name, then calculate the Number of his NAME in Roman numerals which should add up to 666. The number 666 is the number of a man. Therefore, the BEAST is a man, a religious leader.

After knowing the Beast who is a man, then we can find out his name, the number of his name, and the Mark of the Beast and his IMAGE.

The Mark of the Beast has to do with the religious doctrines of this organization that is against the truth in the Scriptures. These are doctrines that are against JESUS and His Ten Commandments.

There are many doctrines that are against JESUS, but two main doctrines that are very evil and are against JESUS, our only God who created us and gave us the Ten Commandments which defines sin. And Protestant Churches including the mainline denominations of the 21st century believed in those two evil doctrines of the BEAST.

1. The Trinity doctrine.

   It teaches that JESUS was not eternal but a creature, a Son of God, born by God the Father in heaven. It teaches three persons in heaven – The Father, the Son, and the Holy Spirit. This doctrine is against the first commandment in the Ten Commandments.

2. The Babies Born Sinners doctrine.

   It teaches that sin is by nature which abolished the Ten Commandments because sin is no longer the transgression of God's law. It teaches that God created baby sinners, baby prostitutes, murderers, fornicators, robbers, drunkards, etc. It teaches that sin is not by choice, but inherited from Adam. This gives one an excuse to sin.

The BEAST is a religious body described in Revelation 13:1-10 where it persecuted believers in JESUS during a period of 1,260 years (538 – 1798 A.D.).

The BEAST is located in Rome, with its headquarters sitting on five hills (Revelation 17:1-10. Scripture gave us the information so that we are well informed and not become deceived.

NOTE: The head of that Roman Organization is the Beast which is Anti-Christ in its doctrines (Daniel 7:17-25).

Listed below are ten (11) false doctrines of the Organization in Rome under the leadership of the Beast in which the devil gave him the power – (Revelation 13:1-3).

1. The Trinity doctrine that says, three persons making up one God.

2. Transubstantiation doctrine,

3. **Immaculate Conception of Mary,**

4. **Sunday is the Sabbath,**

5. **Past, Present and Future sins were already forgiven at Calvary,**

6. **Infallibility of the Church leader,**

7. **Priests can forgive sins of the believers at a Confession box, etc.**

8. **Sin is by nature.**

9. **Sin is without one's choice because we inherited from Adam.**

10. **Babies are born sinners from Adam's sin.**

11. **JESUS who created us is the author of Baby sinners.**

Sad to say that almost all Protestant Churches have accepted the above FALSE doctrines of the Beast.

This is serious. Those false doctrines listed above are Anti-Christ.

CHAPTER 3

WHAT DOES THE BIBLE TEACH ABOUT THE SECOND COMING OF JESUS?

- **The Second Coming of Jesus.**

    o **Every eye will see Jesus.**

    o **The Mountains will shake.**

    o **Every city will be destroyed.**

    o **The <u>dead</u> in Christ will be resurrected.**

    o **The <u>living</u> who are in Christ will be translated.**

. . . .

1. EVERY EYE WILL SEE JESUS DESCEND TO EARTH

Let's read the Scripture:

Acts 1:9-11.

[9] And when he (Jesus) had spoken these things, while they (the disciples) beheld, he (Jesus) was taken up; and a cloud received him out of their sight.

[10] And while they (the disciples) looked steadfastly toward heaven as he (Jesus) went up, behold, two men stood by them in white apparel;

[11] Which also said, Ye men of Galilee, why stand ye gazing up into heaven? this same Jesus, which is taken up from you into heaven, <u>shall so come in like manner as ye have seen him go into heaven.</u>

. . . .

EXPLANATION:

On Thursday night before Jesus died on Friday the next day, he made the promise that he will come again. (John 14:1-3).

On Sunday, Jesus resurrected from the grave. And forty days after the resurrection, Jesus ascended to heaven from the Mount of Olives which overlooks Jerusalem.

While the disciples watched Jesus ascending to heaven, two angels stood next to them and described the manner of his going which will be the same manner as his coming back. This is important. That was **not** a secret rapture.

The disciples saw Jesus ascending. Jesus was not taken secretly.

Remember, the angels told the disciples that the same manner in which Jesus went up, he will return. They saw Jesus ascended and when Jesus will descend, every eye of <u>those who are alive</u> will see him come – Revelation 1:7.

2. THE MOUNTAINS WILL SHAKE AND MOVE WHEN JESUS RETURNS.

Scripture:

Revelation 6:12-17

¹² And I beheld when he had opened the sixth seal, and, lo, there was a great earthquake; and the sun became black as sackcloth of hair, and the moon became as blood;

¹³ And the stars of heaven fell unto the earth, even as a fig tree casteth her untimely figs, when she is shaken of a mighty wind.

¹⁴ <u>And the heaven departed as a scroll when it is rolled together; and every mountain and island were moved out of their places</u>.

¹⁵ And the kings of the earth, and the great men, and the rich men, and the chief captains, and the mighty men, and every bondman, and every free man, hid themselves in the dens and in the rocks of the mountains;

¹⁶ And said to the mountains and rocks, Fall on us, and hide us from the face of <u>him</u> that sitteth on the throne, and from the wrath of the Lamb:

¹⁷ For the great day of <u>his</u> wrath is come; and who shall be able to stand?

. . . .

EXPLANATION

The mountains will shake so hard that the mountains and islands moved out of their places. Wow! That will be a scary time. That does not sound like a secret rapture at all. Who on earth would be found asleep at such a time like that? Surely, everyone will be awake even if it is at mid-night time. This is not going to be a secret rapture event.

Dear reader, when you know the truth, you will easily know the error(s) of the Secret Rapture teaching.

By the way, there is no such thing as a Trinity God is coming back. JESUS is the one returning. He is not a Trinity God. He is not a Triune God.

3. EVERY CITY WILL BE DESTROYED

Scripture.

Revelation 16:17-21

¹⁷ And the seventh angel poured out his vial into the air; and there came a great voice out of the temple of heaven, from the throne, saying, It is done.

¹⁸ **And there were voices, and thunders, and lightnings; and there was a great earthquake, such as was not since men were upon the earth, so mighty an earthquake, and so great.**

¹⁹ And the great city was divided into three parts, and the cities of the nations fell: and great Babylon came in remembrance before **God,** to give unto her the cup of the wine of the fierceness of **his** wrath.

²⁰ **And every island fled away, and the mountains were not found.**

²¹ And there fell upon men a great hail out of heaven, every stone about the weight of a talent: and men blasphemed God because of the plague of the hail; for the plague thereof was exceeding great.

EXPLANATION

The seven last plagues mentioned in Revelation chapter 16 will fall upon the earth before the return of Jesus.

In Revelation 16:17-21 is the seventh plague. This is the last plague and Jesus descends to earth.

Did you read the gravity of the destruction of the cities? Think of cities like – London, Beijing, Moscow, Tokyo, New York, Chicago, San Francisco, Los Angeles, Sydney, Auckland, etc. Freeway overpasses and bridges will crumple down like a piece of paper blown by the wind. Trucks, Buses, Trains, Cars, and passengers will drown. Mountains and islands will move.

Does this sound like there is a Secret Rapture taking place? No way! Think folks.

WHAT IS THE TRUTH?

There is no such thing as a Secret Rapture found in the Bible. It is a misinterpretation of Scripture by Pastors.

Please read the Bible in the context of the plan of Salvation given by JESUS who is our only God (Yahweh / Jehovah) who created heaven and earth in six days and rested on the seventh day (the Sabbath day) – Genesis 1:31; 2:1-3).

WHAT IS THE TEACHING OF "SECRET RAPTURE"?

The Secret Rapture teaching, says:

1. The secret rapture will take place <u>before</u> the time of trouble. The <u>time of trouble</u> is the same as <u>the Great Tribulation time</u> where you cannot buy or sell, as prophesied in Revelation 13:16-18.

2. The believers in Jesus will be taken to heaven secretly <u>before</u> the time of trouble.

3. The non-believers in Jesus will be <u>left behind</u> after the secret rapture event, and <u>they will be on earth during the time of trouble.</u>

4. When the Secret rapture takes place, it will take <u>seven years before</u> the return of Jesus.

5. <u>In the last three and a half years</u> <u>before</u> the completion of the seven years, Anti-Christ will appear in Jerusalem (ISRAEL) to deceive the rest of the people on earth <u>before</u> the second coming of Jesus.

6. <u>The Great Tribulation will be three and a half years before the return of JESUS.</u>

7. Secret Rapture believers teach that we will know the year of the return of JESUS because it will take seven years *after* the Secret Rapture event.

8. IF a plane is flying, and the pilot is a believer in Jesus, he or she will be raptured secretly, and the aircraft will crash. The passengers who are believers in JESUS will be raptured also. People go missing secretly.

9. IF the driver of the car is raptured secretly, then the car will create a crash with other cars, etc.

10. IF the operator of the train is raptured secretly, the train will crash with all the passengers left behind <u>if they are non-believers</u>.

11. IF the wife or husband is raptured from bed, the other spouse is left behind.

That is the teaching of Secret Rapture as believed by many Evangelical Christians and Pastors.

However, when you learn of the truth about the second coming of Jesus in the Chapter after this, you would realize the deception of the Secret Rapture doctrine and wonder, how on earth did they believe in such evil and Satanic teaching?

Many of the ordinary people (church members) are innocent because they did not know how to read the Bible in the context, and they relied on the church pastors to teach them the truth. Besides that, they become so busy in life and had no time to read the Bible, so they entrusted their beliefs to the Church leaders (Pastors). IF they know not the truth because they did not read the Bible, then how do you expect them to know the error(s)? No way they can detect the error(s).

I am praying for whosoever is reading this book to help others know the false teaching (deception) of the Secret Rapture belief (Left Behind Theory).

Let's be very clear. This book is not condemning the people and the Pastors nor the Churches, but the false doctrine called – "SECRET RAPTURE" (Left Behind Theory).

If you as a Pastor are teaching the doctrine called – "Secret Rapture" (Left Behind Theory) before the Great Tribulation period, then it is about time that you restudy Scripture and avoid misleading the people in the congregation. Stop contradicting and twisting the events about the Second Coming of JESUS and the Plan of Salvation.

CHAPTER 4

THE MISINTERPRETED TEXT BY THE SECRET RAPTURE BELIEVERS.

Matthew 24:24-31 is the main Scripture that the advocators of the Secret Rapture teaching got their doctrine from. Therefore, we are going to read the same Scripture and learn for ourselves that there is <u>no</u> such thing as a Secret Rapture. Reading the Bible in the context is very important.

The context in Matthew chapter 24 is about <u>the signs leading to the Second Coming of JESUS</u>. He warned us not to be deceived by false prophets of the last days.

Matthew 24:1-10 (King James Version).

1. And Jesus went out, and departed from the temple: and his disciples came to him for to shew him the buildings of the temple.

² And Jesus said unto them, See ye not all these things? verily I say unto you, There shall not be left here one stone upon another, that shall not be thrown down.

³ And as he sat upon the mount of Olives, the disciples came unto him privately, saying, Tell us, when shall these things be? and what shall be the sign of thy coming, and of the end of the world?

<u>⁴ And Jesus answered and said unto them, Take heed that no man deceive you.</u>

⁵ For many shall come in my name, saying, I am Christ; and shall deceive many.

⁶ And ye shall hear of wars and rumours of wars: see that ye be not troubled: for all these things must come to pass, but the end is not yet.

⁷ For nation shall rise against nation, and kingdom against kingdom: and there shall be famines, and pestilences, and earthquakes, in divers places.

⁸ All these are the beginning of sorrows.

⁹ Then shall they deliver you up to be afflicted, and shall kill you: and ye shall be hated of all nations for my name's sake.

¹⁰ And then shall many be offended, and shall betray one another, and shall hate one another.

. . . .

EXPLANATION

After reading the above Scripture, let us read the Scripture below and see for ourselves if this passage of Scripture gives an indication of a Secret Rapture. You will be disappointed that you cannot find any secret rapture teaching.

SCRIPTURE # 1: MATTHEW 24:24-31.

²⁴ For there shall arise false Christs, and false prophets, and shall shew great signs and wonders; insomuch that, if it were possible, they shall deceive the very elect.

²⁵ Behold, I have told you before.

²⁶ Wherefore if they shall say unto you, Behold, he is in the desert; go not forth: behold, he is in the secret chambers; believe it not.

²⁷ For as the lightning cometh out of the east, and shineth even unto the west; so, shall also the coming of the Son of man be.

²⁸ For wheresoever the carcase is, there will the eagles be gathered together.

²⁹ Immediately after the tribulation of those days shall the sun be darkened, and the moon shall not give her light, and the stars shall fall from heaven, and the powers of the heavens shall be shaken:

³⁰ And then shall appear the sign of the Son of man in heaven: and then shall all the tribes of the earth mourn, and they shall see the Son of man coming in the clouds of heaven with power and great glory.

³¹ And he shall send his angels with a great sound of a trumpet, and they shall gather together his elect from the four winds, from one end of heaven to the other.

. . . .

EXPLANATION

At the second coming of JESUS, the saints (righteous) will be taken to heaven.

There are two groups of people that make up the righteous at the time of JESUS' return.

The righteous that are <u>alive</u> will be taken to heaven. That is the 144,000 mentioned in Revelation 7:1-14 and Revelation 14:1-3. This is the group of people that will be <u>translated</u> like Enoch and Elijah in the Old Testament.

And the righteous that <u>were dead</u>, will be resurrected and taken to heaven as well. These people are <u>not</u> the 144,000 mentioned in Revelation 7:1-14.

This group of people (the righteous dead) are represented by Moses who was dead, resurrected, and taken to heaven by JESUS in the Old Testament.

JESUS is the <u>only GOD</u> (YAHWEH / JEHOVAH) who is coming to take the saints to heaven. HE is the <u>only GOD</u> in heaven. There is no other GOD before him or after him. HE made the promise in John 14:1-3 to come again and take the saints to heaven.

. . . .

THE RETURN OF JESUS IS CLEAR.

SCRIPTURE; 1 THESSALONIANS 4:13-17

[13] But I would not have you to be ignorant, brethren, concerning them which are asleep, that ye sorrow not, even as others which have no hope.

[14] For if we believe that Jesus died and rose again, even so them also which sleep in Jesus will God bring with him.

[15] For this we say unto you by the word of the Lord, that we which are alive and remain unto the coming of the Lord shall not prevent them which are asleep.

[16] For the Lord himself shall descend from heaven with a shout, with the voice of the archangel, and with the trump of God: and <u>the dead in Christ shall rise first:</u>

[17] <u>Then we which are alive and remain shall be caught up together with them in the clouds, to meet the Lord in the air: and so shall we ever be with the Lord.</u>

[18] Wherefore comfort one another with these words.

. . . .

EXPLANATION

1. The dead <u>in Christ</u> will be resurrected and taken to heaven.

2. The <u>righteous believers who are alive</u> at the time of JESUS CHRIST'S return, they will be changed to immortality and taken to heaven. This group is the 144,000 mentioned in Revelation 7:1-14 and 14:1-3.

3. But <u>the wicked</u> who are alive during the second return of JESUS will die and remain dead during the millennium (1,000 years) that followed. They will be resurrected at the <u>second resurrection</u> which is after the millennium, and die the <u>eternal death</u> (2nd death) by the eternal fire when JESUS returns the third time with the New Jerusalem city. (See the chart below). ....

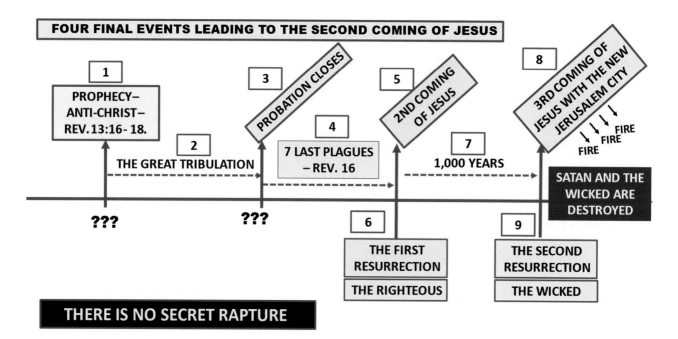

CHAPTER 5

WHY THE SECRET RAPTURE DOCTRINE NEEDS TO BE CONDEMNED?

1. The Secret Rapture doctrine teaches that the year of the return of Jesus can be known. Jesus will return in seven years after the Secret Rapture event. It contradicts the Scripture – (Matthew 24).

2. It is a counterfeit of the return of JESUS to take the saints to heaven.

3. It teaches a false anti-Christ appearing in JERUSALEM, three and a half years before the return of JESUS.

4. It teaches a rapture taking place 7 years before the second coming of JESUS.

5. It teaches a rapture taking place <u>before</u> the Great Tribulation and 7 last plagues.

6. It teaches a <u>False Anti-Christ</u> from the one in Revelation 13:16-18.

7. It teaches a False Beast, a False Mark of the Beast, and a False number 666.

8. It teaches a False Rebuilding of the Temple in Jerusalem.

9. Revelation 16 talks about the Seven last plagues, <u>not</u> Seven last years.

10. Those who advocated the Secret Rapture believed that JESUS abolished the Ten Commandments at Calvary.

11. They also believed that Babies Are Born Sinners.

12. They believed in Sin is by nature.

13. The same people believed that Salvation is unconditional.

14. **The same people believed in the Trinity God – three distinct persons in heaven.**

15. **The same people believed in past, present, and future sins were already forgiven at Calvary.**

16. **They believed that God the Father gave birth to a Son in heaven and called his name JESUS before the angels existed.**

CONCLUSION

The secret rapture teaching came about when people don't really understand the prophecies and the <u>final events</u> leading to the second coming of JESUS in the Book of Revelation.

Of course, the prophecy where you cannot buy or sell in Revelation 13:11-18 is the beginning of the great tribulation period. That event is the cause for the Great Tribulation era which will be followed by the close of probation which marks the beginning of the seven last plagues in Revelation 16. This is <u>not</u> a period of seven years.

Dear folks, don't buy the lie of the doctrine called – "LEFT BEHIND." That is the same doctrine called – "SECRET RAPTURE"

. . . .

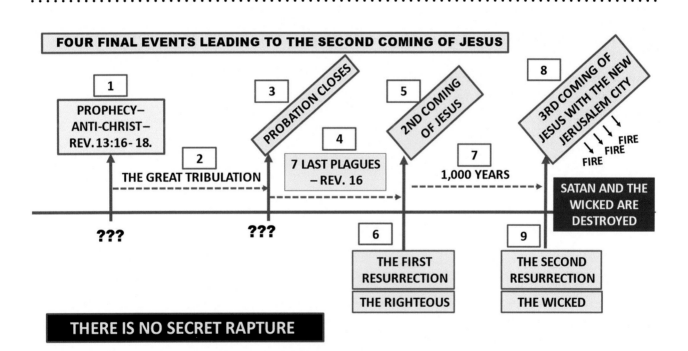

THE "SECRET RAPTURE" TEACHING IS A HOAX

Don't you ever forget this. If the saints have already been taken to heaven by a secret rapture event, then <u>the second coming of JESUS to take the saints does not make sense at all</u>.

Don't buy the lie of the secret rapture teaching from today.

Have a blessed year – 2022, by God's grace.

. . . .

Printed in the United States
by Baker & Taylor Publisher Services